ignite

WINTER SPORTS

SKIING

Patrick Catel

Raintree

Chicago, Illinois

Edited by Adam Miller, Nancy Dickmann,
and John-Paul Wilkins
Designed by Richard Parker and Ken Vail Graphic
Design
Picture research by Elizabeth Alexander
Originated by Capstone Global Library Ltd
Production by Vicki Fitzgerald
Printed and bound in China by Leo Paper
Products Ltd

17 16 15 14 13
10 9 8 7 6 5 4 3 2 1

**Library of Congress Cataloging-in-Publication
Data**
Catel, Patrick.
  Skiing / Patrick Catel.—1st ed.
    p. cm.—(Winter sports)
  Includes bibliographical references and index.
  ISBN 978-1-4109-5452-7 (hb)—ISBN 978-1-4109-
5458-9 (pb)
1. Skis and skiing—Juvenile literature. I. Title.

GV854.315.C38 2013
796.93—dc23   2012042739

Acknowledgments
We would like to thank the following for
permission to reproduce photographs: Alamy
pp. 6 (© North Wind Picture Archives), 10 (© epa
european pressphoto agency b.v.), 11 (© Alaska
Stock), 19 (© Wallis / Photri Images), 28 (© PCN
Photography), 39 (© INTERFOTO), 40 (© George
S de Blonsky), 41 (© ITAR-TASS Photo Agency);
Corbis pp. 8 (Bettmann), 13 (Ales Fevzer), 14
(sampics / Stefan Matzke), 23 (Pawel Kopczynski/
Reuters), 35 (© Giuliano Bevilacqua/Sygma),
36 (Steven G. Smith), 38 (PCN Photography);
Getty Images pp. 4 (Doug Pensinger), 5 (Clive
Mason), 7 (Topical Press Agency), 9 (Imagno/
Hulton Archive), 12 (Kenneth Jonasson/AFP), 16
(Michael Kienzler/Bongarts), 20 (Christof Koepsel/
Bongarts), 21 (Jacques Demarthon/AFP), 22
(Mark Carwell/AFP), 26 (David Hecker/AFP), 27
(AFP PHOTO / Martin Bureau), 30, 37 (Richard
Bord), 31 (AFP PHOTO / Jean-Pierre Clatot), 32
(Alexis Boichard/Agence Zoom); Press Association
Images p. 29 (Sean Kilpatrick/The Canadian Press);
Shutterstock pp. imprint page (© IM_photo),
15 (© Sportsphotographer.eu), 17 (© Beelde
Photography), 18 (© Rob Kints), 24, 25, 45 (©
mountainpix), 33 (© Espen E), 34 (© Martynova
Anna), 40 (© R-O-M-A).

Design features reproduced with permission
of Shutterstock (© Attitude, © twobee, © Rumo,
© Nik Merkulov, © Konstantin Shishkin,
© Rafa Irusta, © Yellowj, © Anna Omelchenko,
© Yarygin, © Nella, © gorillaimages, © nuttakit,
© secondcorner, © Lu Mikhaylova, © R-studio,
© mradlgruber, © mountainpix).

Cover photo of a female skier jumping
reproduced with permission of Corbis (© Adie
Bush/cultura).

CONTENTS

Some words are shown in bold, **like this**. You can find out what they mean by looking in the glossary.

WHAT A RUSH!

Lindsey Vonn is on top of the skiing world in 2010. Now, she is the favorite to win gold in the women's downhill competition at the Winter Olympics. But with the moment approaching, it is uncertain whether she can compete. Two weeks earlier, Vonn injured her right shin. It is painful for her to wear a ski boot, let alone race.

Despite the pain, a determined Vonn is now set to start her run. Can she pull it off? She kicks out of the **gate** with a fast start. Holding a tight stance, Vonn continues building speed. About two-thirds of the way down, she has a scary bobble at a right turn known as Frog Bank. Approaching the finish line, she faces a final jump. Vonn flies about 150 feet (45 meters) through the air in front of the crowd and crosses the finish line. She looks up to the scoreboard and falls back into the snow, raising her arms. She has won!

Lindsey Vonn won the first ever U.S. Olympic gold medal in women's downhill. See page 17 for more about her.

A BRIEF HISTORY OF SKIING

People have been skiing for thousands of years. A 4,000-year-old rock carving showing skis was found in Norway. Skis almost 10,000 years old were discovered in Russia. Written references about 2,000 years old describe skiing in northern China.

Skiing in warfare

In places with snow much of the year, skiing—similar to what we call cross-country skiing—was a useful way to get around the countryside. People hunted on skis and, eventually, skiing was used in warfare.

From warfare to competition

The first competition combining skiing and target shooting happened in 1767, among soldiers along the Norway–Sweden border. In 1861, the first **biathlon** club was established in Norway.

FRIDTJOF NANSEN
October 10, 1861–May 13, 1930

Norwegian explorer Fridtjof Nansen led several expeditions to the Arctic and North Atlantic. He was an excellent skier and, in 1890, he published an account of his journey across Greenland on skis. The book became popular, as did cross-country skiing, and Nansen became known as the father of modern cross-country skiing.

The biathlon combines cross-country skiing and rifle target shooting. When the biathlon was a **demonstration event** at the first Winter Olympics in Chamonix, France, in 1924, it was called "military patrol." The biathlon became an official event at the 1960 Winter Olympics. Women's biathlon was added in 1992.

7

Downhill skiing

Before the mid-1800s, skiing was limited by the **bindings** used to attach the ski to the boot. The earliest bindings only attached the toe to the ski, which made it nearly impossible to ski down steep hills that required turning. Once methods to better secure the heel to the ski were discovered, turning at higher speeds became possible. Soon downhill skiing, or **Alpine** skiing, became possible, with its higher speeds and turns.

NO WAY!

During competitive downhill skiing in California in the 1860s, skiers used 12-foot (3.7-meter) skis with only toe straps—that is about twice the height of a man! Luckily, it was a straight course.

Johan Schneider performs a "jump turn" for spectators in 1946. Lighter, stronger materials and new technology enabled skiers to perform increasingly advanced tricks.

Skiing in wartime

Skiing was used in snowy terrain in World War II (1939–1945). After the war, soldiers spread the sport around the world, and some started ski schools and resorts. Skiing soon grew popular, with more and more people learning.

Ski jumping

Attaching the heel to the ski also meant that ski jumping was possible, since competitors could slow down more effectively. The first ski jumping event took place in Norway in 1879. In ski jumping, competitors ski straight down a steep ramp that ends at an upward-curved takeoff. They try to go as far a distance in the air as possible—it is quite an amazing sight!

MATTHIAS ZDARSKY

February 25, 1856–June 20, 1940

Austrian downhill skier Matthias Zdarsky was a ski instructor and is considered the father of Alpine skiing. In the 1890s, he invented the stem turn, which involves angling the skis to dig their **edges** into the slope, turning frequently in broad zigzags down the hill.

9

ALPINE (DOWNHILL) SKIING

The downhill and supergiant slalom (or super-G) races are single runs down long, steep, dangerously fast courses with few turns. They are considered speed events.

The slalom and giant slalom are considered technical events. Skiers must quickly move and turn to pass both skis through closely spaced gates. The combined race combines the time from one downhill and two slalom races.

Adrien Theaux of France clears a gate during a downhill race at the Alpine Skiing World Cup in Krasnaya Polyana, Russia.

Ski equipment

Early Alpine and **Nordic** skis were made from a single piece of wood. In the 1930s, laminated construction began to be used. In this process, thin layers of material are used above and below the core to reinforce, or strengthen, it. The cores of skis are still sometimes wood. Other times they are foam, which is lighter but not as durable. The layers that go around the core are usually made from **fiberglass** or metal.

New materials, technology, and shapes have allowed Alpine skiers to go faster and jump higher and farther. Luckily, safety equipment is always improving. Recreational skiers, competitors, and skiers filming outrageous video clips now have spine-reinforcing vests, high-tech helmets, and various other pads to keep them as safe as possible in a dangerous sport.

NO WAY!

The average winning speed of international championship downhill skiing events is 40 to 50 miles (64 to 80 kilometers) per hour!

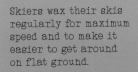

Skiers wax their skis regularly for maximum speed and to make it easier to get around on flat ground.

11

Downhill racing

Downhill and slalom were the original Alpine events. The downhill event is a speed race. Racers must pass through gates that look like a flag between two poles, which are set at least 26 feet (8 meters) apart. Skiers compete one at a time. The shortest time without missing any gates determines the winner.

Downhill is all about speed, with few, widely spaced turns. Whenever possible, skiers tuck into a tight position in order to be more **aerodynamic**, increasing their speed. Downhill's first appearance as an Olympic medal event was in the 1948 games in St. Moritz, Switzerland.

No WAY!

Sweden's Ingemar Stenmark holds the record for most downhill skiing World Cup wins, with 86!

Slalom gates are made of plastic and have springs so that they bend when the skier hits them.

Slalom

Slalom is a race that has more and tighter turns than downhill, which is why it is considered a technical, rather than speed, event. The racer must choose the best line of attack. Speed wins the race, but missing even one gate means disqualification. Men's slalom events have 55 to 75 gates, and women's have 45 to 60.

Slalom was invented by British athlete Arnold Lunn in the early 1920s. The slalom event was added to the Olympics in the 1936 Winter Games in Garmisch-Partenkirchen, Germany.

DAVORIN "DAVO" KARNICAR

Born: October 26, 1962

Some of the most amazing skiing moments are found outside of competitions. In his Seven Summits project, Slovenian extreme skier Davorin "Davo" Karnicar became the first person to ski down the highest mountain on every continent. Davo skied down the final peak of the challenge—Mount Vinson in Antarctica—in 2006.

Giant slalom

The giant slalom event was first included in the Olympics in 1952. With a course longer than the slalom and with wider gates set farther apart, the giant slalom is like a mix of the slalom and downhill. The giant slalom and slalom usually involve two runs held on different courses. The lowest combined time determines the winner.

Austrian Benjamin Raich won gold medals in both the slalom and giant slalom at the 2006 Winter Olympics in Turin, Italy.

torino 2006

NAIL-BITING MOMENT!

Austria's Hermann Maier is known as the "Herminator" because he sometimes seems indestructible. During the 1998 Winter Olympics in Nagano, Japan, Maier walked away from one of the most dramatic crashes in skiing history. He flew 30 feet (9 meters) in the air, landed on his helmet, and crashed through two safety fences at around 80 miles (129 kilometers) per hour. Three days later, he returned and won a gold medal in the supergiant slalom!

Super-G

The supergiant slalom, or super-G, is a
speed event that is the most similar to
the downhill. The course is steep and
straighter than other slalom events.
The turns are not as sharp and are
taken at higher speed. Like downhill,
the winner is the skier with the fastest
single run.

"The last 100 yards I
couldn't even see the
gates. I was skiing on
fumes."

– Bode Miller, 2010, after winning
his first Olympic gold medal

Combined and super combined

The combined and super combined are Alpine ski racing events, although they are not a different type of race. The combined involves one downhill race and two slalom races, in that order. The times are added together, and the person with the fastest time wins.

In 2005, the **International Ski Federation (FIS)** (see page 32) introduced the super combined, replacing the combined. The super combined is made up of a single slalom run and a shortened downhill or super-G run, with the fastest combined time winning. The super combined first appeared in the Winter Olympics at the 2010 Vancouver Games.

NO WAY!

Janica Kostelic is known as "Croatia's snow queen." She has won more Olympic medals than any other woman Alpine skier. Her success did not come without pain: she has had 11 knee operations!

Speed skiing

Speed skiing is an event in which racers try for the fastest speed on a steep, smooth, straight track. The racers use special, shorter skis and wear aerodynamic helmets. Speed skiing is dangerous—several racers have died during the sport.

The FIS wants speed skiing in the Olympic Games. However, the **International Olympic Committee (IOC)** wants to limit the speed of skiers, which is **controversial**. Both men and women in speed skiing have reached speeds greater than 150 miles (240 kilometers) per hour!

LINDSEY VONN

Born: October 18, 1984
Olympic champion Lindsey Vonn won her 50th World Cup race in 2012 and is closing in on the record of 62 for a woman. Still a young woman, Vonn may still have enough time to break Swedish skier Ingemar Stenmark's record of 86 career World Cup victories. Vonn is a favorite to win several medals at the 2014 Winter Olympics in Sochi, Russia.

NORDIC SKIING

Nordic skiing is also called classic skiing, and it is older than Alpine skiing. It is named after the Nordic, or **Scandinavian**, countries where it developed, such as Norway and Sweden. Modern Nordic skiing events include cross-country races and ski jumping, in addition to Nordic combined, which combines results from a cross-country event and ski-jumping event. Nordic events first appeared in the Olympics in 1924.

Cross-country skiing is popular in snowy places, and you don't need a mountain to do it!

Cross-country skiing

There are two **techniques** used in cross-country skiing. In the original technique, the skis are **parallel**, or side-by-side, and the skier kicks backward, creating a gliding motion. In the 1970s, the freestyle technique was developed. Originally called the skating technique, it resembles the motion of ice skating: the skier pushes the inside edge of the ski back and out at an angle. This generates greater speed.

Unlike Alpine skiing, cross-country boots attach to the ski only with a hinged toe piece, so that the heel can move up and down.

You may think of downhill skiing when you hear the word "skiing," but cross-country skiing came first. It was also included in the Olympics 24 years before downhill skiing.

Nordic ski equipment

Cross-country skis are generally longer, thinner, and straighter in shape than Alpine skis, in order to glide on flat snow with little resistance. The boots are a bit lighter, lower, and more flexible than Alpine boots. Ski poles used in cross-country skiing are longer than those used in downhill skiing.

Cross-country ski races

Cross-country racing includes races of several different distances, usually between 6 and 30 miles (10 and 50 kilometers) for men and 3 and 20 miles (5 and 30 kilometers) for women. In most races, skiers start staggered 30 seconds apart, so that they are racing the clock. There is also a relay race involving a team of either four men or four women. In a pursuit race, skiers race against each other in the final part of a two-day event. For racing events, organizers decide which of the two cross-country skiing techniques (classic or freestyle) is permitted in a particular event.

NAIL-BITING MOMENT!

A unique act of good sportsmanship occurred at the 2006 Winter Olympic Games in Turin, Italy. Canadian Sara Renner was in the middle of a cross-country relay that her team was winning when—"snap"! One of her poles broke. Other skiers began to pass her as she slowed. Bjornar Hakensmoen, director of cross-country skiing for Norway, handed one of his ski poles to Renner. The Canadians made up some time but came in second, just barely behind Sweden. Norway finished fourth.

Petter Northug is a famous Norwegian cross-country skier and Olympic champion.

BJØRN DAEHLIE

Born: 1967

Norwegian cross-country skier Bjørn Daehlie, also known as "Rocketman," is perhaps the greatest Nordic skier of all time. Among all winter athletes, he holds the record for the most Olympic gold medals, with 8, and the most Olympic medals, with 12.

Ski jumping

Ski jumping is one of the oldest Nordic skiing events. Along with cross-country skiing, ski jumping has been included in the Winter Olympics since the 1924 Games in Chamonix, France. A second, larger hill was added in the 1964 Winter Olympics, creating a large-hill jumping event.

Most ski-jump championships are contested at 400 feet (120 meters) for the large hill and 300 feet (90 meters) for the normal hill, which represent the distance most skiers could travel from the takeoff and still safely land. Women's normal-hill ski jumping will make its first Olympic appearance at the 2014 Games in Sochi, Russia.

EDDIE THE EAGLE

Born: December 5, 1963

You don't always have to be the best to win fans. In the 1988 Olympic Games in Calgary, Eddie "the Eagle" Edwards became Great Britain's first Olympic ski-jumper. Despite finishing last, Eddie the Eagle won many fans over with his positive attitude.

NO WAY!

Many ski jumpers risk becoming too thin and light in order to gain weight advantage. The FIS introduced a new rule in 2004 that partly links the maximum-length of skis that can be used to a jumper's weight. Since jumpers want the longest skis possible for better aerodynamics in the air, this rule should help prevent ski jumpers from losing too much weight.

Nordic combined and biathlon

The last two Nordic ski events are the Nordic combined and the biathlon. The Nordic combined involves a 6-mile (10-kilometer) cross-country race and a special ski-jumping contest, with the winner based on the most points awarded. The biathlon features the age-old combination of cross-country skiing and rifle shooting (see pages 6–7).

Norwegian Ole Einar Bjorndalen is a famous biathlete.

23

FREESTYLE SKIING

Freestyle skiing combines skiing and **aerial** acrobatics. In recent years, freestyle skiing has expanded in popularity, and new events have been added, such as ski cross and slopestyle. But the main two events that have always been included in freestyle skiing's international competitions are aerials and **moguls**. Ski stunts performed in the air are called aerials. Moguls are the large bumps often found on ski slopes.

Freestyle skis

Freestyle skis are shorter and have greater **sidecut** to allow easier, tighter turns. Mogul skiers generally use softer skis that are better able to absorb shocks. **Twin-tip skis**, which have similar tips and tails, are popular with freestyle skiers who want to ride backward, or "**switch**," such as half-pipe and slopestyle skiers.

Freestyle skiers wear helmets and other padding for safety.

Understanding ski shape

Parabolic skis have a curved shape. When viewed from above, the center, or waist, of the ski is narrower than the tip and tail (front and back ends). The differences in width create the turn radius. The turn radius indicates how tight a turn the skier could make by cutting the ski's edge into the slope to "carve" a turn. It is also referred to as sidecut.

Camber refers to a ski's shape when viewed from the side. When the ski sits on a flat surface, the tip and tail touch the surface, but the waist is in the air. Camber helps press the tips and tails into the snow, creating better edge contact while skiing.

With freestyle and all Alpine skiing, a binding attaches the entire foot (not just the toe) to the ski.

Aerial skiing

In aerial competitions, skiers are judged based on their scores from two jumps, known as "**kickers**." Judges evaluate the takeoff, height and distance, form and technique in the air, and smoothness of the landing. Scores are made up of the following: 20 percent for air, 50 percent for form, and 30 percent for landing. The two types of competition aerials are upright and **inverted** (which means upside down).

A good landing is essential to get a good score from the judges.

The upright competition

In the upright competition, skiers are not allowed to perform any movements where the feet are higher than the head. You will see fun moves like the spread eagle (all limbs extended out while in the air) and daffy (one ski extended forward, the other backward).

No Way!

There used to be another freestyle skiing event called ski ballet, or acro, which was invented in the 1930s. It was more like figure skating than other skiing events. The skier performed a routine set to music, executing spins and jumps on a gently sloping hill. Skiing ballet was dropped as a competitive event after 2000.

Alexei Grishin of Belarus won the gold medal in the men's aerials at the 2010 Winter Olympics.

The inverted competition

Skiers in the inverted competition reach a height of 50 feet (15 meters). After performing several flips and twists, they land on a steep hill. Today's aerial skiers can perform quintuple (five) twisting back somersaults! For safety, aerial skiers practice by using trampolines and by jumping into swimming pools.

Mogul skiing

Mogul skiers navigate around large bumps, called moguls, that are often found on ski slopes. Mogul events take place on a steep course full of these bumps. There are also two upright jumps competitors must hit. Skiers are scored on their speed and technique while turning through the moguls as well as their performance on the two jumps. Mogul skiing was added as an Olympic sport at the 1992 Games in Albertville, France.

ALEXANDRE BILODEAU

Born: September 8, 1987
Canadian freestyle skier Alexandre Bilodeau won the gold medal in the men's mogul event at the 2010 Winter Olympics in Vancouver, Canada. With that win, Bilodeau became the first Canadian to win a gold medal in his home country. Bilodeau's hero is his brother Frederic, who suffers from a disability called cerebral palsy. Alexandre has used his ski fame to raise money for cerebral palsy research.

Ski cross

Based on snowboarding's snowboard cross event and using the same course, ski cross is a head-to-head race. Each ski cross race has either four or six starters. The first skier across the finish line wins. Ski cross is considered a freestyle event, even though it is more of a downhill discipline.

The course is designed to test all of the skills a great skier might have. Course features include a variety of turns and jumps, flat and rolling sections, and banks and ridges. It is an exciting event, with skiers dangerously close to one another and little room for error.

Hometown girl Ashleigh McIvor (center) won a gold medal in the women's ski cross event in the 2010 Vancouver Games—the event's first Olympic appearance.

Slopestyle skiing

Slopestyle and half-pipe skiing events have grown in popularity along with the Winter X Games. Both events will be featured in the Olympics for the first time in 2014 in Sochi, Russia.

Slopestyle courses offer options, with a variety of jump and **rail** choices at various spots. Skiers are judged on the creativity and difficulty of their **line**, the tricks they perform on the features and off jumps, and the **precision** of their landings. Skiers maneuver both forward and backward.

"Slopestyle getting into the Olympics is a super cool opportunity for the sport. I was already excited about half-pipe, but this brings our sport full circle into the mainstream media and the biggest sporting event in the world."

Torin Yater-Wallace, 2014 Winter Olympics hopeful who became the youngest Winter X Games competitor and medalist in 2011, at the age of 15

From left to right, silver medalist Tom Wallisch from the United States, gold medalist Bobby Brown from the United States, and bronze medalist Andreas Hatveit from Norway pose after the men's ski slopestyle final at the Winter X Games Europe in 2012, in Tignes, France.

Half-pipe skiing is very dangerous. Sadly, Canadian half-pipe skier and Olympic medal hopeful Sarah Burke died in a half-pipe training accident in 2012.

Half-pipe

A half-pipe is a course shaped like a half cylinder dug into the hill. The half-pipe used in Winter X Games and international competitions is a superpipe—a very large half-pipe. The Olympic superpipe is 550 feet (167 meters) long by 60 feet (18 meters) wide, with 22-foot- (6.7-meter-) high walls. Both snowboarders and skiers use the same superpipe.

Skiers speed up the side of the pipe, fly out over the rim, perform aerial tricks, land back in the pipe, and ski across the bottom to the other side for the next trick. In Olympic half-pipe, seven judges give one overall score based on **amplitude** (height out of the pipe), difficulty of run and use of the pipe, and variety and execution of tricks.

MAJOR COMPETITIONS

Aside from the Winter Olympic Games every four years, the biggest ski competitions are the World Championship, the Ski World Cup, and the Winter X Games. The Ski World Cup and Winter X Games happen every year. The Ski World Championship happens every two years.

Governing body

The International Ski Federation (known globally as the FIS) is the world governing body of competitive skiing. The FIS makes the rules for international competition and approves event courses. It was founded in 1924 during the first Winter Olympic Games in Chamonix, France. Today, the FIS has 110 National Ski Association members.

"It's good to ski for fun, but I still want to win races as often as possible."

– Hermann Maier, Austrian skier

Alexis Pinturault of France is focused during the Alpine Ski World Cup men's slalom in 2011 in Alta Badia, Italy.

World Ski Championships

The FIS holds a World Ski Championship every other year, in odd-numbered years. This includes both an Alpine and Nordic World Ski Championship, with all the usual events in each.

Leading up to the Olympics, skiers compete in **sanctioned events** to earn points and an international standing, which determines their entry into the Olympic Games. The 2013 FIS Alpine World Ski Championships were held in Schladming, Austria. The 2013 Nordic World Ski Championships took place in Val di Fiemme, Italy.

NO WAY!

Kjetil-Andre Aamodt of Norway is the most decorated racer in Alpine skiing history, with 20 medals. He won 8 Olympic medals (four gold, two silver, and two bronze) and 12 World Championship medals (five gold, four silver, and three bronze).

World Cup

The FIS recognizes a World Cup for cross-country skiing, but the FIS Alpine Ski World Cup is more famous. It has been awarded every year since 1967 to the top male and female Alpine skiers. The winner is the skier who receives the most points in downhill, slalom, giant slalom, super-G, and super-combined events at FIS-chosen competitions throughout the winter season.

Apart from the chance at an Olympic gold medal, many consider the World Cup the most coveted prize in skiing, since it tests a skier's skills in a variety of races throughout a whole season. The winner of the Ski World Cup receives a crystal globe trophy. The World Cup season starts at the end of October in Soelden, Austria, and finishes in March in the Alps or in Scandinavia.

Maria Hoefl-Riesch celebrates after winning the FIS Alpine Ski World Cup event in Sochi, Russia, in February 2012.

ANNEMARIE MOSER-PRÖLL

Born: March 27, 1953

Although American Lindsey Vonn is catching up, Austrian Annemarie Moser-Pröll holds an all-time record, with six women's World Cup championships. Five of the six she won five years in a row, between 1971 and 1975. Moser-Pröll has won three Olympic medals, and she also holds the record for career World Cup event wins, with 62. It probably helped that she has been skiing since she was four years old!

Recent Alpine World Cup winners

Year	Men	Women
2012	M. Hirscher (Austria)	L. Vonn (United States)
2011	I. Kostelic (Croatia)	M. Riesch (Germany)
2010	C. Janka (Switzerland)	L. Vonn (United States)
2009	A. L. Svindal (Norway)	L. Vonn (United States)
2008	B. Miller (United States)	L. Vonn (United States)
2007	A. L. Svindal (Norway)	N. Hosp (Austria)
2006	B. Raich (Austria)	J. Kostelic (Croatia)
2005	B. Miller (United States)	A. Pärson (Sweden)
2004	H. Maier (Austria)	A. Pärson (Sweden)
2003	S. Eberharter (Austria)	J. Kostelic (Croatia)

Winter X Games

The "X" in X Games stands for "extreme," as in extreme sports. The first Winter X Games was televised in 1997. It featured early snowboarding and the first half-pipe, which was half the size of today's superpipes! Today's Winter X Games includes several skiing events: big air, slopestyle, superpipe, and ski cross. Of these, only big air has yet to make it into the Olympics.

For the big air contest, skiers take a long approach, building speed for one really big jump that sends them far through the air. It is almost like a ski jump, but with aerial tricks! The most amazing tricks that are consistently landed determine the winner, based on a combined score from two runs.

David Wise won ski superpipe gold at the 2012 Winter X Games— the first American to do so since Tanner Hall in 2008.

36

> "I feel good. But then I see Kai [Mahler] almost land a switch double misty 1620 ...Everyone's at such a high level now that no one person is that far above anybody else."
>
> – Skier Bobby Brown, in 2012, after winning his second Winter X big air gold medal

NO WAY!

In the 2012 Winter X Games ski slopestyle competition, Canadian Kaya Turski became the first woman to land a switch 1080 in X Games history. "Switch" means that she started the trick riding backward. The number "1080" means that she turned completely around three times in the air before landing (there are 360 degrees in each full rotation).

Canadian skier Kaya Turski won gold for the third year in a row in the women's ski slopestyle at the 2012 Winter X Games.

WINTER OLYMPICS

The first Winter Olympic Games were held in 1924 in Chamonix, France. Originally the Summer and Winter Games were held the same year. Starting in 1994, the Winter and Summer Olympics began to alternate on even-numbered years.

The 2010 Winter Olympic Games were held in Vancouver, Canada. The 2014 Winter Games will be held in Sochi, Russia, and the 2018 Winter Games will be in Pyeongchang, South Korea. Because of the cost and amount of work the Olympics require, host cities must be chosen well in advance.

NO WAY!

In the opening ceremony of the 1994 Games in Lillehammer, Norway, Stein Gruben brought the Olympic torch into the stadium riding down a ski jump! He had to take over and perform the stunt after Ole Gunnar Fidjestol, who had been planning it as the last jump of his career, injured himself in a practice jump.

Competition was fierce in the ski cross competition at the 2010 Vancouver Games.

Olympic ski history

The International Ski Federation (FIS) was founded in 1924, the same year as the first Winter Games. At first, Nordic skiers resisted the inclusion of Alpine events in the Games. However, in 1930, the Nordic skiing countries of Norway, Sweden, and Finland withdrew their complaints, and the FIS approved Alpine events. Alpine skiing made its Olympic debut at the 1936 Games.

The 1936 Winter Olympic Games were held in Garmisch-Partenkirchen, in Germany.

JULIA MANCUSO

Born: March 9, 1984

Rivaling Lindsey Vonn in women's Alpine skiing is American teammate Julia Mancuso, who has three Olympic medals and four World Championship medals. Mancuso has the most medals of any woman Alpine skier in U.S. Olympic history. She hopes to continue her Olympic success at Sochi in 2014.

Paralympic Winter Games

The first Paralympic Winter Games took place in Örnsköldsvik, Sweden, in 1976. Cross-country skiing and two Alpine events, the slalom and giant slalom, were included. The Games now include cross-country and biathlon, as well as four Alpine events: downhill, super-G, slalom, and giant slalom.

Paralympic skiers include those with a physical disability such as a spinal cord injury, cerebral palsy (which affects body movement), amputation (a missing limb), visual impairment, and a group called *les autres* (those with conditions that affect body movement).

Athletes with physical disabilities use equipment that is adapted to their needs, including a single ski, sit-ski, or orthopedic aids.

Keeping it fair

The **International Paralympic Committee (IPC)** has 13 classes for Paralympic Alpine skiers: seven for standing, three for sitting, and three for visually impaired athletes. A specific system of calculating results allows athletes with different impairments to compete against one another and still ensure that competition is fair. Just like the Olympics for the able bodied, winning is determined by skill, fitness, power, endurance, and focus.

NO WAY!

In 2010, Jessica Gallagher became the first Australian woman to win a Winter Paralympic Games medal, claiming bronze in the women's slalom for the vision-impaired. Skiers with visual impairments are guided through the course by sighted guides who use voice signals to indicate the course to follow.

The Sochi Olympic logo is revealed during a ceremony in Moscow's Red Square. Sochi, Russia, is host city for the 2014 Winter Olympic and Paralympic Games.

QUIZ

How much do you know about skiing?
Test yourself with these questions.

1. Where will the 2014 Olympic Games be held?
a) Vancouver, Canada
b) Turin, Italy
c) Sochi, Russia
d) Nagano, Japan

2. What does "super-G" stand for?
a) supergiant slalom
b) super gravity
c) super girl
d) super games

3. Is ski jumping a Nordic or Alpine skiing event?
a) Nordic
b) Alpine

4. Which two of the following are considered technical Alpine skiing events?
a) supergiant slalom
b) slalom
c) downhill
d) giant slalom

5. Which two of the following are considered speed Alpine skiing events?
a) downhill
b) slalom
c) supergiant slalom
d) giant slalom

6. Which two of the following ski events will be included in the Winter Games for the first time in 2014?

a) half-pipe
b) slopestyle
c) big air
d) biathlon

7. In skiing, "moguls" refer to which of the following?

a) rich, powerful people
b) furry animals found on ski slopes
c) aerial tricks
d) large bumps often found on ski slopes

8. Which of the following is NOT a freestyle skiing event?

a) ski jumping
b) aerials
c) moguls
d) slopestyle

7–8 correct answers: Clearly, you know your stuff when it comes to skiing! Perhaps you could be competing for medals in the future.

4–6 correct answers: Not bad. Try to join a club in your area and get some practice in.

1–3 correct answers: There is so much to learn about skiing. Try to watch some on television or on the Internet, and see if you can learn more about it. You might find you want to try skiing yourself!

Answers

1. c
2. a
3. a
4. b & d
5. a & c
6. a & b
7. d
8. a

43

GLOSSARY

aerial acrobatic maneuver performed in the air

aerodynamic using the principles of aerodynamics, which studies how objects move through the air; an aerodynamic object moves smoothly, with less resistance, through air

Alpine relating to mountains; Alpine skiing is downhill skiing

amplitude in half-pipe skiing, amplitude refers to the height or distance the skier reaches in the air, out of the pipe

biathlon skiing event that combines cross-country skiing and rifle shooting

binding platform skiers use bindings to attach their boots to their skis

camber refers to the curved shape of the ski when viewed from the side, like a bow shape

controversial subject that leads to divided opinion and public disagreement

demonstration event Olympic events are first tested as demonstration events before becoming official medal events

edge thinnest side part of the ski that cuts into the hill when carving a turn

fiberglass light, strong material made from glass threads pressed together

gate two plastic poles with a flag in between, which racers must maneuver around in ski events; gates have springs so that they bend

International Olympic Committee (IOC) governing body of the Winter and Summer Olympic Games

International Paralympic Committee (IPC) governing body of the Winter and Summer Paralympic Games

International Ski Federation (FIS) Fédération Internationale de Ski; world governing body of skiing

inverted upside down

kicker short, angled jump that shoots a skier straight up into the air

line path a skier chooses down a slope

mogul large bump often found on ski slopes

Nordic referring to Scandinavian, or Nordic, countries, such as Norway, Sweden, and Finland; Nordic skiing, in which only the toe is attached to the ski, includes cross-country skiing and ski jumping

parabolic in the shape of a curve; a parabola is like the curved shape made by the path of an object thrown high into the air to land a short distance away

parallel side-by-side in the same direction

precision state of being accurate or exact

rail metal bar with a flat or rounded surface that a skier can slide across

sanctioned event event that has been officially approved by the FIS

Scandinavia area of northern Europe that includes Norway, Sweden, Finland, and Denmark

sidecut determined by the difference in width of a ski's waist (center) compared to the tip and tail; also referred to as turn radius or sidecut radius, sidecut determines how tight a turn a skier can make by cutting the ski's edge into the slope

switch riding backward on skis

technique special way of doing something that requires a lot of skill

twin-tip ski ski where the tip (front end) and tail (back end) are almost identical, which makes it easier to ride backward

FIND OUT MORE

Books

Champion, Neil. *Wild Snow: Skiing and Snowboarding* (Adventure Outdoors). Mankato, Minn.: Smart Apple Media, 2013.

Gifford, Clive. *Skiing* (Get Outdoors). New York: PowerKids, 2011.

Hudak, Heather C. *Skiing* (Extreme). New York: Weigl, 2009.

Web sites

espn.go.com/action/blog/_/sport/xgames
This is the home page for the X Games, where you will find the latest information concerning the Winter and Summer X Games.

www.fis-ski.com
This is the official web site of the International Ski Federation (FIS), where you will find information about athletes and the latest results from international ski contests.

www.nsf.gov/news/special_reports/olympics/aerialskiing.jsp
This web site of the National Science Foundation includes a video on the science behind twisting techniques used in aerial skiing.

www.olympic.org
This is the official web site of the Olympic Games, where you can find information about past and future Olympics, as well as famous Olympic athletes.

www.paralympic.org
This is the official web site of the Paralympics, where you can find information about past and future Paralympics and Paralympic sports, as well as famous Paralympic athletes.

ussa.org
This is the web site of the U.S. Ski and Snowboard Association (USSA). It is the national governing body of Olympic skiing and snowboarding. This site is full of useful information about everything going on with skiing and snowboarding in the United States.

DVDs

Classic Ski Films (6 DVDs) (Topics Entertainment, 2009).

A History of Ski Films: 70 Years of Thrills, Chills & Spills. Directed by Greg Stump, Dick Barrymore, and Otto Lang (Topics Entertainment, 2011).

Warren Miller's Children of Winter: Never Grow Old. Directed by Warren Miller (Shout! Factory, 2009).

Warren Miller's: Playground. Directed by Max Bervy (Shout! Factory, 2008).

Places to visit

Lake Placid, New York
www.whiteface.com/index_w.php
Located in the Adirondack Mountains in New York, Lake Placid hosted the Winter Olympics twice, once in 1932 and once in 1980. It is known for its Nordic and Alpine ski terrain.

Salt Lake City, Utah
saltlake2002legacy.com
Salt Lake City hosted the 2002 Winter Games. Located in Utah just west of the Rocky Mountains, Salt Lake City is close to several great ski resorts, including Alta, Brighton, Snowbird, and Solitude. The area often gets huge amounts of dry, powdery snow.

Squaw Valley, California
www.squaw.com
Located in Olympic Valley, California, Squaw Valley Ski Resort was the site of the 1960 Winter Olympics. It is the second-largest ski area at Lake Tahoe, in the Sierra Nevada mountain range.

U.S. Ski and Snowboard Hall of Fame and Museum
610 Palms Avenue
P.O. Box 191
Ishpeming, Michigan 49849
www.skihall.com
Located in Ishpeming, Michigan, this museum in the Upper Peninsula has a large collection relating to the history of skiing. While you're in Ishpeming, you might be able to catch a ski jumping competition at Suicide Hill!

INDEX